ISBN: 978-1499250305

Printed in the United States of America

To Gammy,
who's made me fear failure since the day I was born.

# SHUT UP AND TWEET

@ PHIL PALLEN

# TABLE OF CONTENTS

# INTRODUCTION

"If you've got a big mouth and you're
controversial, you're going to get attention."

@SimonCowell

I know you're interested in this whole "Twitter" thing. It's the reason you're looking at this book.

You're intrigued and you *should* be. Last year alone, Twitter had over 100 million daily active users.[1] But I've never been one for statistics, so enough of that. I'm more enticed by tangible things that affect me day to day, like growing my influence or bank account. For me, Twitter plays a crucial role in accomplishing both.

Maybe you're the person who tried Twitter and stopped. Perhaps you just don't know where to start. Regardless of

[1] Matthew Panzarino, "The Twitter IPO By The Numbers," *TechCrunch*, tcrn.ch/1mLr1lx

who you are or where you're from, buckle down and get ready to do Twitter the right way.

Have excuses? I've heard them all. Any of these look familiar?

> "What's the point?"
> "I don't care what people are eating for breakfast."
> "No one would want to follow me."
> "Privacy is important to me. I'm not comfortable being on display like that."
> "Twitter is for teenagers, not businesspeople."
> "I don't have time."
> "It's just not for me."

Well, shake every hesitation and excuse right out of your head. They won't work here.

You can state every possible reason as to why you shouldn't tweet, but guess what? If you want to be smart about growing your brand and business on the Internet, you really don't have any choice.

Twitter is here to stay, so embrace it. As the saying goes: If you can't beat 'em, join 'em.

But in this book, we don't just join 'em, because most of 'em are doing it all wrong. And we're not just going to talk about it—you're going to learn the right way to get significant results.

So, get acquainted with your new mantra: Mistakes are

better than nothing. A half-assed tweet trumps no tweet at all. The longer you stick with your new game plan, the better you'll get. This book is like learning to ride a bike, except the bike will get you seen by millions of people.

If you don't have time to read (my go-to excuse), never fear. This book is short, just like my attention span. Every effort has been made to keep it lean, fun, and brimming with just the good stuff. It's easy to become overwhelmed with Twitter, and I've been there myself. When you're done here, the things you found confusing about Twitter won't be confusing anymore.

Full disclosure: I'm not a wet blanket like the majority of the social media experts out there. I've achieved success through consulting because my approach marries branding with intelligent social media strategy. No one wants to be smart and ugly, or beautiful and stupid.

Without further ado, meet your new Bible (or Richard Dawkins book) made from the fruits of thousands of hours on Twitter. I love the platform and soon you'll love it too. (And me, but that's a given.)

Shut up and tweet.

Love,

SHUT UP AND TWEET

# CHAPTER ONE:
# #BIGBUCKS

"Change is such hard work."

@BillyCrystal

Simply put, Twitter holds the keys to your brand's potential. Your audience is sitting there waiting for you to reach out to them. Don't believe me? Let the numbers spell it out for you: 72 percent of Twitter users following small-to medium-sized businesses are more likely to make a purchase after following the company. Not only does your Twitter following impact purchasing decisions, but the power your brand holds on a follower lingers. A jaw-dropping 82 percent of Twitter users are more likely to recommend the brand to friends after following them online.[2] That's a lot of referrals.

---

[2] Douglas Ethé-Sayers, "Market Probe International and Twitter Announce Small and Medium Business Twitter follower Insights," Market Probe International, Inc., marketprobeint.com/index.php/press-twitter

Convinced? I certainly hope so. If not, reread the paragraph.

A few years ago, I got a call from a California realtor, Amy, who specialized in luxury beachfront homes in Los Angeles. Her clients were wealthy, yes. Tech savvy? Probably not. I'd assumed that they were too busy enjoying the likes of retirement to fuss around with a computer.

Amy wanted a new logo designed for her business cards and property signs. Before committing to the project, I asked her a very important question:

> *Phil*: "What's your brand?"
> *Amy*: "What do you mean?"

And in that moment, I knew a logo was just one piece of the puzzle for Amy. After chatting about the importance of building a brand, she decided to explore social media as a way to promote her business.

Keep in mind—Amy had never tweeted before. Not once.

After four months of chipping away to build her Twitter presence, Amy received a tweet from a new follower inquiring about a current listing on her new website. Within a week, Amy had a multi-million dollar sale. Not bad for a novice tweeter.

Although I was excited for her, I wasn't surprised. Amy did everything right. She quickly caught on to the fact that Twitter is not the proper medium for sales pitches, even though many people use it that way. If you're blatantly selling on Twitter, you've got it all wrong.

Authenticity is rare these days. From the moment we wake up, we're the targets of marketing. TV and radio ads are the more obvious examples. How about the branded pens in your desk drawer, or the magnets on your fridge? It's happening all around us, all the time, and we've become experts at shutting it out. Just like with the boisterous oversharer at the office, we reciprocate with a nod, a nervous grin, and a secret plan to get the hell out of there. There's nothing worse than a one-sided conversation, and sadly, that's the harsh reality for most traditional marketing.

This is not the case with social media. Its rise to everyday consciousness was born from the fact that consumers——people like you and me—call the shots now. (Take that, advertisers.) In fact, 78 percent of consumers say they trust peer recommendations[3], which includes social media channels, whereas only 14 percent say they trust advertisements[4]. If you don't like a certain brand, don't follow them. Problem solved. And if they still try to get to you after you've already decided you don't like them, well… Nod, grin nervously, and get the hell out.

At the end of the day, if a brand is going to earn your

[3] Stacey Miller, "Fifty Essential Social Media Marketings Stats," Vocus, vocus.com/blog/essential-stats-social-media-marketing

[4] Erik Qualman, "39 Social Media Statistics to Start 2012," Socialnomics, socialnomics.net/2012/01/04/39-social-media-statistics-to-start-2012

follow, they better be sharing top-quality content that makes it worth your time and effort.

So, what was Amy doing right on Twitter? She knew that it was a means of staying on other people's radars and being authentic. Not once did she tweet, "Look at my listing! Buy my listing!" Regardless of her motive, that would come off as desperate, and desperate isn't cute. Instead, she sent just a few tweets each day. Amy engaged her followers in conversation by sharing relevant information and, most importantly, she effectively reached complete strangers she wouldn't normally connect with. Her audience received a daily reminder that Amy is an expert with an opinion, not a salesperson.

Don't underestimate your audience. They aren't all 12-year-old girls tweeting about boy bands. In fact, the 55- to 64-year-old age bracket is the fastest growing demographic on Twitter[5]. Users are savvy communicators seeking genuine connections. And unsurprisingly, 85 percent of customers expect businesses to be active on social media[6]. That's a massive group that you don't want to disappoint, so never talk down to them with a one-sided sales pitch.

You can't have a business without an audience, so you've got to treat them right. Contribute to their day in a

---

[5] Belle Beth Cooper, "10 Surprising Social Media Statistics That Might Make You Rethinnk Your Social Strategy," The Huffington Post, huffingtonpost.com/belle-beth-cooper/10-surprising-social-medi_b_4325088.html

[6] "Meaningful Brands – Havas Media launches global results," Havas Media, havasmedia.com/press/press-releases/2011/meaningful-brands-havas-media-launches-global-results

positive way by sharing a quote or tidbit of valuable information. Heck, tweet something they'll see and think, "I can't think of a better way to say it myself!" That'll land you a retweet.

Let's imagine you're shopping in your favorite clothing store. You walk in and take your time to browse around. You're open to purchasing, but only for something really special. Finally, you see it: The shirt of your dreams. The shirt of all shirts. You grab it, touch its soft and lustrous fabric, and you think to yourself, *This is it. This is what I want to be buried in.* You try it on and it's perfect. You step out of the fitting room to look for a bigger mirror, when suddenly a sales associate starts following you around like a starving parasite and badgers you with a pitch.

"That color really brings out your eyes!"
"It looks sooo great on you!"
"It's really slimming!"
"Did you know we also have that in canary yellow?"
"Want to sign up for our store's credit card for 10 percent off?"

You know the drill: nod, grin nervously, and get the hell out. Say goodbye to the shirt.

We've all been there. Someone assumed you were a single-celled organism and you didn't like that. No one likes to be told what to do or what to feel.

Now think about the last positive experience you had in a

store. The sales associate wasn't pushy. She didn't follow you around. Didn't pester you to the point of discomfort. Rather, she was helpful. You felt open to asking questions and, based on her knowledgeable responses, you knew that she was familiar with the store's inventory. There was trust and a genuine connection. And you more than likely visited the store again, even if you didn't buy something the first time.

*That's* what you need to deliver to your followers.

One important thing to note: If you're looking for direct return on investment (ROI) from Twitter or any social media channel, you might as well put this book down. Yes, 60 percent of U.S.-based small businesses find that social media helps them gain new customers, but that's not the point[7]. Social media is not a sales tool; it's a relationship-building tool that often leads to sales. There's a major difference. Whenever a prospective client brings up the expectation of direct sales from one of our initial calls, it's a red flag for me. I don't take on clients like this. Social media is about sharing information and experiences, not sneaking into someone's wallet or purse and wringing their bank accounts dry. When you're trustworthy and good at what you do, the money will follow.

Recall those one-sided traditional marketing methods I ranted about? You've probably already gathered that I'm not a big fan. Another unappealing truth is that they

---

[7] "Priming the Economic Engine: How social media is driving growth for small and medium businesses (SMBs)" LinkedIn, business.linkedin.com/marketing-solutions/c/14/2/smb-research-whitepaper.html

typically cost money. A *lot* of money. Social media is a gem for lean marketing budgets because the costs to reach targeted audiences are often minimal if you're strategic. Platforms like Facebook and LinkedIn allow you to advertise—and make an impact—for just a few dollars a day. Even better, Twitter allows you to access a targeted audience for FREE.

Let me explain using a comparison to traditional marketing. A billboard on Sunset Boulevard can run you $100,000 per month and that's not even taking into account the amount you'd spend securing that spot against competition. You and I both know that billboard advertising doesn't lead to immediate sales. No one sees a retail ad on a morning commute and U-turns to the nearest shopping mall. The call to action (CTA) doesn't have instant payoff, and advertisers readily accept that.

But why do they still spend thousands per day to show you that visual? They do it to build brand awareness. To stay on your radar.

Your tweets do exactly the same thing, except they're free. When you make a connection with someone, it lasts. You stay on their radar on your terms, instead of hoping that they don't zone out while driving or watching TV. Twitter is all about meaningful relationships.

And multi-million dollar sales.

# CHAPTER TWO:
# #TAKEFLIGHT

"As far as I'm concerned, Twitter has wiped out Facebook. I'm done with Facebook."

@KevinOLearyTV

Before you begin your journey to Twitter stardom, remember that the platform truly lives in its own universe. You could be a Facebook marketing genius and have absolutely no idea how to approach Twitter. (It happens more than you think.) There's a completely different set of strategies you'll need to use to get noticed. There's a language and tactics that the strong use to survive.

Let me make myself clear—Twitter is *not* like Facebook. Throw out everything you know about Facebook because you're playing for a new team, and the mascot is a bird... not a stylized F.

Facebook represents your close-knit friend group (and

family, assuming they haven't blocked you). When a complete stranger tries to add you, it's like a nosy unknown barging into your private conversation; you ignore that request—and quick. Why would a complete stranger want into your personal life? Creep.

Twitter is not this way. In fact, it's almost entirely the opposite. Strangers will "follow" you (not in person... if they do, call your local law enforcement office immediately) and that's exciting! It's like building your very own fan base. Your first break to stardom. They're following you because they like what you have to say, even if they don't know you. Major compliment.

I often liken Twitter to an airport—a hub where people from all different places move in all different directions. They've got unique goals and a common purpose: to get somewhere. It's a prime people-watching destination. Sometimes people are boring. Sometimes they're terrifying and you hope to God you're not seated next to them on the plane. But sometimes, if circumstance welcomes it, you have a great conversation with someone, and you remember them.

When I say Twitter leads to genuine relationships, I'm not making that up to impress you. I've met many of my favorite clients through Twitter. Within minutes of following my client Branden Hampton, our direct messages led to emails, a phone call, a spankin' new website, and an invoice.

It was all very simple, really. I liked what Branden had to

say, he liked what I had to say, and we found a way to work together. It's a genuine connection out of common interest and admiration. You can have that with someone who follows you, too.

(Side note: Branden is a complete genius. He caught onto the Twitter game early and his username is—I kid you not ——@CEO. Now he's getting paid to send out tweets because he owns extremely valuable Twitter real estate; his social media accounts have 31 million followers combined[8]. That's basically the population of Canada. Ironically, we've positioned his brand as the ultimate slacker.)

Unlike Facebook, Twitter defines you less by your "activity" and more by what you put out into the world[9]. Your tweets will have a sooner expiration date than your Facebook posts, but if you share thoughts of quality (note: *not* what you cooked for breakfast, unless you're Wolfgang Puck), people will look forward to your musings on a regular basis.

Be proud of your thoughts and don't be scared to share them. Use a unique perspective to your advantage and show it off to the Twitterverse.

---

[8] Matt Brian, "Meet the man who makes six figures a quarter just from using Twitter," The Next Web, thenextweb.com/twitter/2013/02/07/building-a-business-from-twitter-meet-the-man-behind-the-accounts-you-see-every-day

[9] By the way, if you're going to use Twitter to its fullest potential, don't keep your profile "private." I totally get why that makes sense on Facebook, but as far as I'm concerned, it shouldn't even be an option on Twitter. Otherwise, what's the point? No one will see it. You are what you "tweet," and if you've got secrets no one should know, keep them to yourself. Simple.

# CHAPTER THREE:
# #FIRSTIMPRESSIONS

"Sometimes you can't see yourself clearly until you see yourself through the eyes of others."

@TheEllenShow

I have to break some terrible news to you.

Every single day people judge the way you look. At the grocery store, the office, on the street. People judge.

Just as a prospective friend, employer, colleague, teacher, or whomever immediately scrutinizes the way you look and speak, the exact same thing happens on Twitter, but faster. It's not that they want you to fit a mold or status quo. They just have high expectations, as they should.

Make sure your profile represents you.

There are so many components to Twitter aesthetics that I could write a whole book on them. (Foreshadowing?) For the sake of your reading experience, I'm going to quickly run through the different parts of your profile and what's needed to make them work.

## Handle

Choosing a Twitter handle (username) is unexpectedly tough, given that each one needs to be unique. It can—and should—require a lot of thought. Just when you think of the perfect Twitter handle, you'll be hit by the rude reality that someone beat you to it. It will feel like your perfect Twitter handle is taken, and that's because it probably is. Time for some creativity!

My client Michelle is the CEO of the largest women's conference in the US. She regularly travels across the country to speak in front of thousands of people. Despite repeatedly promoting her handle (@MJNPatterson) to conference attendees, few actually remembered it. So we changed it.

After many rounds of brainstorming, we arrived at @ItsMeMichelleP, an adorable rhyme that's hard to forget. Now she's growing faster than ever because people can easily find her.

When choosing a Twitter handle, ask yourself these questions:

## 1. Who does this Twitter handle represent?

It may be you as a personal brand, a representative of a company brand, or as the company brand itself. That's up to you and the flexibility you'd like to have.

## 2. I have more than one brand. Should I have more than one Twitter account?

Have the smallest number of accounts possible. Consolidate and you will be grateful in the long run. I get that it's not always possible to juggle two distinct brands. (Imagine the problems bouncing between a skydiving instructor and life insurance company.) Every handle doubles your workload, which is not the best use of time given the other worthwhile social media platforms you could also be using.

## 3. Is my name unique enough for its own handle?

If it is, lucky you. Maybe people can't pronounce it, but it's your best friend on the Internet. Scoop it up on Twitter if it's available. While you're at it (if you haven't already), visit your preferred Internet domain registrar (like GoDaddy, 1&1,

name.com, etc.) and purchase your name domain, even if it's just a placeholder[10].

## 4. How can I make my name unique on Twitter?

If you're set on using your full name and your name is ordinary, *please* don't just reserve a handle with a few numbers tagged on the end. (You'll never see me use @philpallen2349, for example). That will make me sad. But most importantly, it will reduce the chances that someone will remember your handle long enough to follow you. A common name isn't necessarily a bad thing; you'll just have to get clever. Maybe try:

- Adding "the" to the front (like my trusty sidekick @thelaurenmoore).
- Using a verb at the end, like "tweets" or something specific to your line of work.
- Trying a funny rhyme using your first name.
- Integrating your name into another word or phrase (like my friend Kyle, who uses @picodekyo to rhyme with pico de gallo salsa).
- Starting with "iam, "ask," or "its".

The easier to remember, the better.

---

[10] Don't worry about the add-ons the domain registrars will sell you; however, domain *privacy* is good to have——otherwise, web users can look up the home address associated with your domain. Sounds like the beginning of a murder mystery.

## 5. Should my Twitter and website address be consistent?

Yes. Your Twitter handle should match all of your digital real estate. If someone visits your URL (yourcompany.com, for example), they should be able to search on Twitter and find @yourcompany. Try your very best to be consistent. It helps in the long run. The fewer handles people need to remember, the better the chance they'll follow you across multiple social media platforms.

For the record, you can change your Twitter handle if you need to without losing the empire you've built (under settings), but I don't recommend doing that often. People are slow to catch on to change. Decide on a brand handle and commit to it. If it's available, it's all yours[11].

### Bio

Almost everyone has a terrible Twitter bio.

When it comes to establishing a brand, your bio is one of the most valuable and underused assets on your profile. It's highly visible digital real estate. Let me remove the guesswork and teach you how to write your Twitter bio.

---

[11] Unless you undergo the terribly rare fate of Naoki Hiroshima, who possessed a coveted single-letter handle @N. It was supposedly worth $50,000 and was thus stolen by a Twitter hacker. He ended up getting it back, though. And lived happily ever after.

This strategy is very simple and it will work for you, not against you.

It all comes down to two sentences:

> First: Tell me who you are and why I should care.
> Second: Show your personality.

I practice what I preach because it works. At the time I write this, my bio on Twitter reads:

> "Brand and social media strategist for TV personalities, public figures, and entrepreneurs. If your baby is ugly, it's my job to tell you."

My Twitter bio is a tool to grow followers and strike up conversations. Most people laugh at it. Some find it offensive, which is a sure sign they won't like my tweets. Most importantly, people pay attention. I get tweets from people specifically about my bio on a daily basis.

Your bio doesn't have to be comedic, by the way. Sass and brutal honesty are defining attributes of my brand, so they are amplified in my bio. Dr. Sanda Moldovan is a client of mine whose bio is more professional:

> "Award-winning periodontist and nutritionist as seen on @TheDoctors. If the eyes are the windows to your soul, then the mouth is the gateway to your health."

See what she did there? The first sentence provides much-needed context and credentials. The second shows her mantra and approach to her job. Bam. Everything said that needs to be said and under the 160-character limit.

Here's another example of a client bio that says it all:

> "I build stars – songwriters and artists like @SherylCrow, @JewelJK and @MichelleBranch. We start with a song."

I'm sure you're catching on here. Writing your Twitter bio isn't like getting a tattoo, by the way. It's as permanent as you want it to be, and given the medium, a switch every now and then is beneficial. If you've got a product launch, special event, or exciting news altogether, incorporate it into your bio. Just don't forget to take it out when the news is over[12].

Remember this: Your Twitter bio is much like an advertisement. It's the first place people will look for more information. Every Twitter user you follow (with enabled notifications) will receive an email saying you followed them, along with your display picture and bio. Will they follow you back or not? This is the ultimate moment of judgment. Be smart, be clever, be unique, and then you can sit back as all the followers and tweets roll in.

---

[12] When I change a client's Twitter bio to include something time sensitive, I set a future reminder in my calendar to change it back to the original when the promotion is over. This offsets the risk that they'll have a bio about Halloween at Christmastime.

## Location and Website URL

This section is very straightforward, yet many people seem to royally screw it up. Your location is the city you live in, not "Everywhere" or "Universe." Obviously you don't have to put your exact address, but at least put your city down as an anchor. It's there because many people do searches to find users in their area. Location is a nice thing to have in common with a prospective client or customer.

List your brand, company website, or blog as the URL on your profile[13]. Put your best foot forward and send users to the appropriate place to find out more about you. They *will* check it out if they're enticed by your profile. Notice that it's "link," singular. Don't go cramming multiple URLs here or in your bio because it always looks sloppy. As I've preached before, this isn't a sales pitch. Besides, people are only going to go to one place. Don't confuse them with choices.

## Profile Photo

Oh, the profile photo. So much potential and so many letdowns.

The first step is to replace that god-awful default egg thing Twitter automatically assigns new accounts. Get rid of it. I never want to see it. If you refuse to change it, put the book down.

---

[13] If you don't have either of those, why are you reading this book? Did you come for the jokes? Welcome to the Internet. Now get a freaking website.

Choose a new picture and get it up there ASAP. This is your moment to dazzle potential new followers with your sexy mug. The better you look, the more likely people will follow you. You don't have to be a supermodel, but just look your very best. Not a pixelated photo from your family reunion five years ago. I suggest using a professional photo with proper lighting. You likely won't get it done for free, but it's well worth the investment. Why? This is the substitute for your facial expressions in real life. It accompanies every single tweet you'll send. Look fun, natural, and energetic. Make a strong first impression[14].

Your photo needs to crop nicely into a square, so focus on the face and forget the torso. Don't be afraid to crop in fairly close, too. Most people taking a gander at your profile will be on their phones, which means everything is small. Test out a few options. A second opinion never hurts.

---

[14] I've put together a summary of how to prepare for a professional photo session on my blog. Visit philp.al/gp101

## Profile Design

Twitter is constantly updating its design to keep things fresh. As a result, the elements you can customize are also changing. I wish I could refer to specifics, but Twitter will probably update the interface before I can finish my thought. My advice is to keep things clean and minimal. This is the adult version of your high school locker. It speaks volumes about you to complete strangers, so decorate with caution. Use the customized photo opportunities to showcase your personality and keep the custom colors consistent with your website and brand.

## CHAPTER FOUR: #LEARNTHELINGO

"I'm not motivated to entertain people through Twitter, so just by having Twitter and not saying anything, I make people mad."

@louisck

Looking at a Twitter feed for the first time feels like visual Morse code. In fact, these questions ran through my mind:

What's with the bird?
Who is RT?
Why can't I post on someone's wall?
Where ARE the walls?
Why is someone following me?

Good thing I'm about to clear that up. Here's a refresher on the basics.

**Tweet**

This is a public record of statement published from your Twitter account. It's a thought, a question, a fact, an update, a hyperlink, or any other form of blabbing textual information in 140 characters or fewer. Not surprisingly, tweets make up everything that is Twitter. Go to Twitter.com, type something into the search bar, and take a gander at the buzz about that topic; tweet after tweet after tweet.

**@Reply**

A way of responding to someone who has tweeted you. At first glance, it's a grammar freak's worst nightmare, but I've broken it down for you to put those syntax stresses to rest.

Imagine having a real-life conversation with, say, me. It goes something like this:

> *Phil*: I hope you're enjoying *Shut Up and Tweet*.

> *You*: I am! I can't put it down, because it's the best thing I've ever read.

Not so bad, right? Just a normal conversation between two (relatively) normal people. Now imagine this is happening on Twitter. My handle is @philpallen and, for the sake of simplicity, let's assume yours is @you. Here's what it would look like:

*@philpallen*:
I hope you're enjoying *Shut Up and Tweet*, @you.

*@you*:
@philpallen I am! I can't put it down because it's the best thing I've ever read.

See what happened there? A normal conversation just like the one above, but you moved my name to the front of your reply[15]. That way I know you're speaking directly to me and I'm notified about it.

And you, my good friend, just did an @reply.

## Mention

Revisit the Twitter conversation between @philpallen and @you. Do you see how my first tweet to @you has the username at the back? Including someone's username, like in this scenario, is called a mention.

It's also worth mentioning (pun intended) that you can use most punctuation, like periods, commas and question marks, normally without it interfering with your mention or @reply. By design, these characters are not allowed to be used in Twitter names. The only character you'll see used in

---

[15] For intermediate Twitter users out there, did you know that starting a tweet with an @reply hides it from everyone else's feed? Twitter interprets @replies as something only those two people need to know about. If you want your response to be seen by the public, integrate their handle into your reply, like starting off with "Hey @philpallen." Lazy people will just put a period before the handle, but I don't because I'm not *lazy*. Neither are you.

handles is an underscore ("_"), which you wouldn't need anyways.

## Retweet

You'll likely come across tweets that make you think, "I couldn't say it better myself!" Don't worry, you don't have to. Give it a retweet to automatically send it out to your followers so the person who said it first gets credit.

Put some time and effort into your tweets and you'll notice people retweeting you too. It's the ultimate social media compliment.

Pretty basic so far, right? Until now, because there are *two* different kinds of retweets. Each serves a distinct purpose. Before you panic, let me explain.

### New-Native Retweet

Ever heard a really good joke from your super witty friend that you're dying to retell? New-native retweets do that. They attribute the author so you aren't accused of being a joke stealer. Basically, everybody wins.

New-native retweets are integrated into Twitter's platform. Below anyone's tweet you'll see "retweet" listed as an option to click. When you retweet this way, the tweet is shared in its original form, uninterrupted. You can't modify or add anything;

all you do is pass it on, so to speak. This form of retweet includes everything from the original (including the creator's profile photo and handle) and displays it in your personal Twitter feed. The only difference is the small line underneath that says "retweeted by," which explains why the heck your followers will see a tweet by someone they likely aren't following[16].

When would you want to put the native retweet function to work? Great question. It works best when you're:

- Giving a stamp of approval to something you saw.
- Sending a stronger message about a cause or piece of news, like something breaking on CNN.
- Wanting a tweet to go viral (funny GIF or one-liner? Go for it).
- Being ironic.

See the new native retweeting possibilities? Endless.

A word of caution: Never overdo it. You'll look lazy and we all know how much I disapprove of that. Do you want to be known as the person who always borrows everyone else's opinion? Didn't think so.

---

[16] Unless you're retweeting Oprah. Everyone follows Oprah.

Since this retweet type is in the bag, onto the next:

**Old-School Retweet**

The original. Old-school retweets go way, way back to when Twitter was developed in 2006, coined by its early adopters.

Back to the scenario board. Pretend I tweeted this out:

> *@philpallen*:
> I love my book, *Shut Up and Tweet*.

Before Twitter built the new-native functionality, retweeting me would look like this:

> *@you*:
> RT @philpallen I love my book, *Shut Up and Tweet*.

That's it. All you do is copy my tweet, plunk an RT in front of it and send from your account. A cinch.

Let's say you want to add a little something of your own:

> *@you*:
> It really is the best! RT @philpallen I love

my book, *Shut Up and Tweet*!

> Same deal as last time. Copy and paste my tweet, add a little RT, and this time plop in a note of your own at the very front. You're adding your two cents.

Imagine you want to retweet my original book love tweet and add even more thoughts, but your words in addition to mine push this tweet over the 140-character limit.

Enter:

## An MT

Modified tweet. This is a special form of retweet and not as common. It's still giving due credit and usually shortens the original so that it fits within the 140-character limit.

For example.

> *@you*:
> I'll never forget the first time I read *Shut Up and Tweet*. It was simply magical. MT @philpallen I love my book!

Make sense? If my original tweet had been left intact, you wouldn't have been able to publish anything because it'd be too damn long. My original tweet was shortened to just "I love my book," and MT was used after your reply instead of RT. I'm still getting credit for the original and you're able to give your two cents in full.

Let's move on.

**Via**

So much of Twitter is about sharing. It's important to give props when appropriate. Inserting "via" into your tweet before sharing a link is a great way to do this. Imagine that you want to share the joy of *Shut Up and Tweet* by tweeting a link to the Amazon purchase page[17]. You could do something like this:

> *@you*:
> Check out this amazing book, everyone! via @philpallen philp.al/shutuptweet

Easy, right?

For now, that's all you need to know. Of course, there's this thing called Google that you can use whenever you're stuck or if you want to learn more. But for now, you've got the tools to properly converse.

I know this chapter is technical, but what you've learned is essential. I'm glad we got through it together.

---

[17] You should totally do that, by the way.

# CHAPTER FIVE:
# #CONTENTMACHINE

"I hate to talk about myself."

@KimKardashian

When you go to a party, the last thing you want is to be stuck next to a dull person who has nothing original to say. It's the same on Twitter. Don't be boring. Bring something interesting to the conversation.

Of course, there are some chatty people at parties who take things way too far. There's the Wall Street bro who only talks about his workplace successes. The ditzy girl who would be much better off saying nothing. The downer in head-to-toe black who's genuinely concerning. I could go on.

You are not a party stereotype. You're an expert. A dynamic, insightful individual with brilliant thoughts about a variety of topics. And once you start tweeting, the whole world is going to know that too.

I'm about to let you in on one of Twitter's best kept secrets:

Twitter is a tool for conversation, not for broadcasting.

It represents opportunity. Every single tweet you publish is an instant billboard impression. You'll have access to thousands of people who just might care about what you have to say. It may seem daunting, but as long as you be yourself, everything's going to be great. That's the most positive thing I've said so far. Savor it.

Media is now democratized. Before, you needed serious degrees and credentials to be respected in the industry. Now everyone is waving "look at me!" and indulging in self-created content on their blogs and social channels. But that doesn't mean it's high quality. In fact, I believe content is in infinite supply on the Internet. Everyone's doing it and for that reason it becomes increasingly difficult to get noticed.

If you think about it, we're all competing for one thing; a few seconds of attention. If content is unlimited, time has become the valuable currency that we're all after.

Let it be known that you'll never win them over with content alone. With the likes of Google, Yahoo Answers, and eHow, rest assured the information people desire already exists. I don't mean to burst your bubble, but your idea is probably not original. It's out there. Can't find it? Look harder.

So if it's not content alone, what's the missing ingredient to your secret sauce? Personality. No one can survive with content alone. I would argue that every person's appeal comprises a unique ratio of content to personality. Everyone's ratio is different.

Look at Martha Stewart. Her success comes from pioneering do-it-yourself (DIY) content before we could find it plastered all over Pinterest. Martha's lack of personality is outweighed by an extensive knowledge of domesticity. Now I'm sure that Martha's friends and family know her in a different way than the public does (and who knows, maybe she can crack a joke or two), but at first glance, we're more likely to take interest in Martha because of her expertise, not personality.

On the opposite side of the spectrum, Ellen DeGeneres has built a global brand stemming from her personality. People don't watch her show for hard news. They want her spin on pop culture. More serious subjects, like her passion for animal rights, came to light once she earned a loyal fan base.

I explain this ratio to TV hosts, experts and entrepreneurs: When you are the product you're trying to sell, be aware of what you're offering. Be in tune with your strengths and weaknesses so you can fairly assess the best opportunities. This is especially important when you're publishing content on a daily basis.

The content creation techniques I'm about to teach you aren't recycled from another social media publication. I created my tweet type system out of necessity. People have no problem learning about revamping their Twitter presence, but when it comes to applying it, they're stumped. Yes, I want the overall content quality in the Twittersphere to improve (those auto-tweets *have* to go), but I also want to help you methodically tackle your social media output. If it's organized, it's easier to execute. Ideally, it becomes integrated into your daily routine.

When it comes to quantity, bite off what you can chew. As you'll see, there are four tweet types in total. Ideally, you should rotate between these four tweet types equally, with at least one type per day. This ensures that you have a refreshing mix of content that's in your voice.

To those who can whip up four daily tweets like it's nothing, great. Do one tweet type per day. To those who feel like I just asked them to climb Mt. Everest, I promise you that it's a lot easier than it looks. Whether you tweet once a day or ten times a day, the key is to be consistent. Choose a daily number and do whatever you can to stick to for as long as possible. Now keep reading before you get cold feet.

To keep this simple and memorable, I assign a two-letter short form to each tweet type. Do whatever it takes to relate these to your brand. Jot 'em down and fill these margins with notes for all I care.

## Website Link (WL)

This tweet can be anything that's self-promotional, or anything about you. A link to your blog or maybe some recent press coverage. It's better if there's a link associated with what you're posting. If it's just a comment, I engage with your brand for the time it takes me to read it and then I'm off to something else. If there's a link and you're sending me somewhere to get more information, I could potentially engage with your brand for a lot longer. Use this.

The majority of tweeters send out just this tweet type and that's it. Selfies aren't going to grow your business. Stop embarrassing yourself. Even if you're the central topic, give people some variety.

## Quick Question (QQ)

Self-explanatory and meant for engagement, this tweet type has only text and no link. If we're aspiring to converse, not broadcast, the content you share needs to engage your followers. What's the point of having an audience if you're not going to interact with them? I use this tweet as a way to stay on people's radar and collect valuable feedback. Your quick question should always be specific. If you leave it open-ended, people are more likely to ignore it. It can be "on-brand" in the sense that it refers to something related to your product or service, or it can be completely unrelated. Both are okay, as long as they're interesting and relevant to a good portion of your audience.

Let me give you a recent example that's on-brand for me. Before deciding on the cover artwork for this book, I posted the final four contenders on Twitter and Facebook to gauge people's reactions. I explicitly asked people, "What design do you like best? 1, 2, 3 or 4? Comment below." In less than an hour, I accumulated hundreds of responses. It's the most popular Facebook post I've ever had. The reason? I gave the audience specific parameters as opposed to an open-ended question. I wasn't asking for an essay, just a quick preference that required minimal effort on their part. There was no room for confusion and my audience did what I told them to do[18].

Quick questions don't always have to be about the industry you work in. I'll give you another example of a good non-brand related quick question. How about something as simple as tweeting, "Coffee or tea?" at 8am (when some of us are awake and probably don't want to be)? Now sit on that for a second. This question applies to a huge number of people. You're being relevant and direct without sounding robotic.

Keep in mind, the more you grow your followers, the more likely you're going to have people interacting. If you only have 30 followers, only 30 people will see your tweet. I'll teach you how to grow your audience later, but it starts with good content.

---

[18] I love when people do what I say.

**Industry Buzz (IB)**

Take this opportunity to establish your credibility as an expert. You're an expert, right? *Right?* I don't care if you've been in business for a hundred years or if you started yesterday: if you're going to be successful, you need to be viewed as an expert. That needs to translate on Twitter, so it could be a statistic, a fact, or a small piece of advice— anything that reminds us, wow, you really know what you're talking about. On my Twitter account, I share lots of information related to social media (news, trends, advice) because that's my brand and I know what my audience wants. Build the credibility you need for people to take you seriously.

People always forget how qualified they are as an expert. You probably have the tendency to opt for humility, when in reality you're far above the status quo. I'm not just trying to stroke your ego here: When you're wholly devoted to your career, chances are you know far more than the average Joe. I tell my clients to record their phone calls (creepy, yet effective) and play it back to themselves after it's done. Try this and take notes. When you're done, you'll have a slew of industry buzz tweets ready for publishing.

## Networking Effort (NE)

This is the *most* important type. It's the foundation of what Twitter is all about. When you work hard to expand your network, you're going to have thousands of people following you on Twitter and you're not going to know most of them. And that's okay. It's perfectly normal, actually. You need to make an effort to build that network, find complete strangers, and form a connection. Use whatever means you're comfortable with (Google, Twitter search, magazine articles, to name a few options) and send them a tweet saying what you like about them. A compliment goes a long way. From experience, I can tell you that this transforms complete strangers into long-term clients.

Avoid being self-promotional. Let's revisit our Twitter-like-an-airport example: If I aggressively shove my business card in someone's face, that person is either going to ignore me or scream. Whatever the reaction may be, it won't be positive.

In application, maybe try this: Tweet, "I read your article in this magazine and I love your perspective." People love public praise. Even if they won't retweet it, they'll likely reply or favorite it[19]. Now they've noticed you and you're on their radar. You've started a conversation and it could go somewhere exciting.

---

[19] A subtle nod of approval, in Twitter speak.

## CHAPTER SIX:
## #POPULARITYCONTEST

"Some people change when they think they're a star or something."

@ParisHilton

You could have the best Twitter profile in the world, but that doesn't mean people will know you exist. You have to do a bit of chasing (or following, in this case) to get the grand prize: a booming audience.

As far as I'm concerned, Twitter is the best free outlet for accessing a targeted audience. Every other platform has some sort of restriction, whether it's a pending friend request, an ad campaign, or a dollar out of your pocket[20]. Not here. It's time to tap into the potential of your network without spending a dime.

---

[20] I consider spending money a restriction. I like it to stay in my bank account.

In some ways, Twitter is a popularity contest. The more followers (people subscribing to your tweets) you have, the cooler you seem. Likewise, if you're following thousands of users but have very few following you back, people will wonder why no one wants to hear from you. To be a rockstar in this world, you have to give a little to get a lot, which means marginally increasing your following count[21].

Actively following Twitter users is the primary reason my clients organically grow from a few hundred followers to many thousands of real followers. It's possible to purchase followers on Twitter. Sure, they'll add to your follower count, but they won't do anything like interact with you or buy your product. They're purely for vanity's sake, which can sometimes have a purpose[22]. But let's not focus on that right now. I want you to connect with *real* people. Buying followers won't necessarily achieve that and it certainly isn't free.

It's all about following people who will be excited by what you have to say. Of course, it's a bit more complicated than that, so I've created a foolproof plan to help you out.

---

[21] If you aren't a celebrity, you probably won't accumulate thousands of followers while only following a small handful of people. It just doesn't work that way for us mere mortals, so be open to increasing your following count.

[22] In a negotiation, for example. I once worked with a children's toy company and my client had a meeting with a huge retailer. He wanted to give the retailer the impression he had an established following, when he did not. He bought followers and made the deal because the buyer was convinced there was demand. The power of manipulation.

## 1. Accept that you're using Twitter differently from now on.

This is the beginning of a new era. Your days of using a Twitter timeline like a normal person are over. (I'll explain why as we go through the steps). This isn't a second version of Facebook or a high school reunion; this is a *business tool*.

Come to terms with this and say goodbye. Let's move on.

## 2. Utilize Twitter lists.

You're going to need a way to filter out the noise as your account grows, which it will. That's where lists come in.

It's rare to find someone who uses this Twitter feature effectively. Lists allow you to preserve the accounts you genuinely care about, whether they follow you back or not. The chance of getting a follow from Kim Kardashian is slim, but if you add her to a list, you'll still get her tweets without having to follow her.

So add your favorite celebrities, your crazy aunt, Chipotle, and anyone else you like to a list. Once they're on there, you'll receive their tweets on your timeline just like you did before, but without wasting a precious follow on their account.

## 3. Unfollow everyone who isn't following you back.

If someone isn't following you but you're following them, get over it: It's a one-way relationship and you're not benefitting from it. Dump them and move on. When someone earns a follow from you, they need to cherish it.

I want you to keep your followers as high as possible and your following as low as possible. This means some unfollowing needs to be done.

There are lots of services out there that can help you with this next part. I'm not going to give you specific names because they're constantly changing. Tweet me for my most recent pick or Google the phrase "Twitter unfollow not following back". The basic necessary functions you'll need from this tool are:

> 1. The ability to unfollow anyone who isn't following you back.

> 2. The ability to copy followers of another Twitter account.

> 3. Most importantly, the ability to track how many users you have followed through this tool.

Once you get the right service for you, unfollow everyone who isn't following you back. Every single one of them.

## 4. Make a list to copy followers.

Assuming you want to grow your targeted follower base, we first need to locate where they are. Let's pay attention to these three important groups of people:

> *Competitors*: Other companies in your market who are vying for your customer's attention. If they sell what you sell, they're direct competitors. If they sell something different that satisfies the same need as your product, they're indirect competitors. Both are important to identify (and crush).

> *Like brands:* They accomplish or care about the same things as you. They may be similar in some ways, but they're not competing against you for market share. They could be in a different region or be a not-for-profit company related to your product or service.

> *Brand heroes*: These brands do what you do, but they're a few steps ahead. Sometimes they're nationally recognized

SHUT UP AND TWEET

or operating at a global level (like Whole Foods or Disney). They usually have quantity in their favor, which is helpful for this exercise.

Make a list of Twitter handles from brands spanning these three groups. In fact, do it right now. We'll call this your hit list[23].

_____

_____

_____

_____

_____

_____

_____

_____

_____

[23] I was a little nervous to use this name, but then I remembered my liability clause.

_____

_____

_____

_____

_____

_____

_____

_____

_____

_____

_____

_____

_____

_____

_____

We're about to make an assumption for all of these groups. Given that people are following these accounts that are positioned similarly to you, their followers may be interested in what you have to say too.

## 5. Start following people.

Once you've unfollowed everyone who isn't following you back, look at your hit list[24]. I want you to copy the first 300 followers of the first Twitter handle on there. Do *not* follow more than 300. Twitter sets a limit to prevent suspicious bot activity and will suspend your account.

## 6. Interact with people who tweet you.

You're going to notice a lot of Twitter activity, which is exciting. If someone tweets you, start a conversation with him or her. Look at their Twitter profile and make a remark about their bio or a recent tweet they sent out. Have fun with it and see what happens.

Note: Please don't set up an account that sends out automated thank-you tweets to everyone who follows you. It is so, so tacky. You'll surely be on

---

[24] Again, liability clause.

the receiving end of this, so ignore them. #punishment

**7. Repeat.**

Wait a few days, and start from the beginning: Unfollow everyone who isn't following you back, then copy the followers of the second person on your list.

Continue this for eternity, adding to the list as needed.

I need to emphasize just how effective this method is. It's my bread and butter so only share this with people you like. And certainly keep it from your enemies. You'll sleep better at night knowing that you have a major proprietary advantage over them.

Sweet dreams.

# SHUT UP AND TWEET

# CHAPTER SEVEN:
# #RIPPLEEFFECT

"I'm very much about letting other people shine, because it makes us all shine brighter."

@chelseahandler

Now that you know what to tweet and how to grab people's attention, we're going to kick it into high gear and turn those ripples into tidal waves.

You've heard the term "viral"—Gangnam Style, Rebecca Black, your favorite Super Bowl commercial. When content becomes worthy of sharing, it spreads like wildfire. It sounds easy. It's anything but.

Viral content may take the form of cute, funny, or stupid on the surface, but at its core it's got to be contagious. Those who are able to successfully achieve viral status have created content that elicits a discussion-worthy reaction. Otherwise, why share it?

Keep this in the back of your mind with every tweet you send, especially your networking effort tweets.

Major brands will do whatever it takes to be personable. Once I tweeted about a BMW marketing campaign that I thought was killer, and sure enough, @BMW retweeted me. Don't hesitate to communicate with these brands. More often than not, they'll acknowledge you.

I know this game from both sides. I'm there personally when tweeting brands like BMW, but I'm also the gatekeeper when it comes to many of my celebrity clients. I often decide what gets tweeted, retweeted, or ignored. Take my advice: Think like the influencer. If you're the diamond in the rough tweeting something specific and positive about their brand, they're more likely to share it with the world. Common sense, really.

For your followers, write your tweets in a way that's retweet-friendly. Oftentimes the most successful tweets I've sent out on behalf of clients are extremely direct. A tweet like this:

RT if you've read *Shut Up and Tweet*!

Will more likely be RTed than one like this:

I'm reading *Shut Up and Tweet*!

And that's for a reason. With so much activity going on in your followers' feeds, sometimes a direct command is what gets you ahead. That way it's mindless. Like I've said before, less effort means a happier follower.

Don't overdo it. If you've got a funny comment or opinion with zero call to action, put it out there. Every audience is different. Test out various ways of communicating messages and see which ones best stick with yours. Use those cues to develop a brand voice for yourself that's effective for your audience.

Here's something different: One time, I had a client who wanted to do something meaningful using his eager audience. He decided to send out a tweet guaranteeing a small donation to his favorite charity for each RT. You wouldn't believe the response in such a short period of time.

Sometimes, people will be warm, fuzzy, and welcoming to you in the Twitter world. Other times, people will be bullies. It's a fact of life.

If you're a business owner, you might get someone complaining about a recent experience they had as a customer. Don't ignore them unless they're obscene or really inappropriate. They tweeted you because they want a resolution. Give them a way to contact you and treat them right. Don't write anyone off without giving them a chance.

# CHAPTER EIGHT:
## #LIKEABOSS

"As long as you're going to be thinking anyway, think big."

@realDonaldTrump

You know the tweet types. You've probably scribbled down future ideas. But putting it all together can be overwhelming.

Forty-six percent of web users look to social media before making a purchase. That's a lot of future customers you want to entice[25]. You must give your platforms purpose. For Twitter, ask yourself what a follower can expect from you in one sentence. If you can't narrow it down, think long and hard before putting anything out there. For example, my goal on Twitter is to meet and communicate with new people by sharing my insights on social media

---

25 "How Connectivity Influences Online Shopping," Nielson, nielsen.com/us/en/ newswire/2012/how-connectivity-influences-global-shopping.html

and branding.

If you don't know your purpose, you can't position yourself for growth. You'll just have friends and family following you to be nice. Do you want to get two likes on a picture from Grandpa's Easter brunch or do you want to share a thought-provoking *Fast Company* article that gets retweeted 30 times? Think of your business and brand goals before personal ones.

You might worry that putting such a firm label on your platform could hinder your ability to produce content, but that's incorrect. I can assure you that this exercise will give you the focus necessary to program properly. In fact, having such rigid standards for your Twitter content will *help* you. Part of why people have such irregular posting patterns on Twitter is because of the seemingly infinite posting possibilities. Now you have an easy way to decide whether an idea fits the bill or should be tossed aside.

This rule should apply to all of your social media platforms. Each outlet needs an individual focus that specifically caters to the platform and the type of user. For example, I couldn't apply my Twitter goal to my Pinterest account. It just wouldn't work. Pinterest is all visual; it's not nearly as timely as Twitter. Because of that difference, I use Pinterest for another purpose: to document great examples of branding[26].

---

[26] Need inspiration for your branding? Check it out. It's the second-best thing to hiring me. pinterest.com/philpallen

So figure out each platform's purpose and stick to it. Regularity and persistence will get you results.

Now it's time to create your own content calendar. This is the big leagues! If you expect to get thousands of loyal followers by tweeting once per day, good luck. You're an industry expert now and people need to hear from you regularly. Have higher standards than that.

Keep in mind: This shouldn't be a painful process. If writing your posts feels like taking out the trash, they probably are trash. Don't treat tweeting like a chore because you'll avoid it. Be as silly, far-fetched, creative, or serious as you'd like to be. This is your outlet, your tool for expression.

There are many social media management systems (SMMS) out there and they are our friends. Many are either free or affordable. These systems allow you to input tweets and often schedule a time for that post to publish. And since Twitter engagement for brands is 17% higher on weekends, you'll want to plan those tweets in advance so your social life doesn't suffer[27]. That's not the way I like to live and I'm certain you don't want that either.

My pick for a social media management system is Buffer. I've tried them all, and Buffer wins[28]. Another popular

---

[27] Belle Beth Cooper, "10 Surprising New Twitter Stats To Help You Reach More Followers," Buffer, blog.bufferapp.com/10-new-twitter-stats-twitter-statistics-to-help-you-reach-your-followers

[28] They should pay me to promote them. (They don't.)

choice is Hootsuite. Most of these management dashboards offer free monthly trials so I recommend testing out a bunch to see which work best for you.

Plan your tweets in advance. The last thing I want is for you to get up in the morning and slap together something half-assed.

Here's an idea: Post evergreen content. Evergreen simply means it's relevant at any time. Instead of planning "How's your Saturday going?" schedule "How's your day going?" That way you can shuffle posts as necessary and not risk coming across as a complete idiot if it posts on a Wednesday.

I'm going to teach you how to monitor your progress, which ensures you continue to do the right thing and fix mistakes. Computers track platform growth and statistics to make our lives easier.

On the first of every month, use your SMMS's reporting tool to analyze the previous month's performance. There will be information on how to do this online or you can always message an account rep who will gladly show you what to do. Take note of your most popular tweets. Then ask yourself these questions:

- Which tweets did people respond to?
- Which were favorited?
- Did I get more retweets when I wrote RT in the copy?

Objectively analyze your content and disassociate all emotions while doing so. If your funny joke didn't fly, it doesn't mean that you have a crappy personality; it's just not meaningful to your audience. After a while, you'll notice commonalities among your most popular content. There will be a certain tone to them, a subject area, a length, *something* that ties them all together. Once you've figured that out, you'll know what to keep writing for future posts.

Another important thing to do is track your link click-throughs. Services like Bitly shrink a URL to save character space. But it gets better: Bitly links also track how many people click on them! This gives you a huge advantage when determining what content to share.

How do you track clicks per Bitly link? Great question. Simply copy and paste your Bitly link into an address bar and then add a "+" sign at the end of your URL[29]. You'll see all click-throughs and when they happened.

The hard part is over. Congratulations. The information needed to ensure total Twitter domination is now in your brain. You have the tools necessary to succeed.

---

[29] This isn't limited to your links. You can do this for any Bitly link. It's a great way to creep on how successful, and unsuccessful, major brands are on Twitter.

# CHAPTER NINE:
# #ITSAWRAP

"You don't learn to walk by following rules. You learn by doing, and by falling over."

@richardbranson

Remember, there's no way to screw up if you're just being yourself. Be excited about it. I'm excited for you.

By the way, the fun doesn't have to stop here[30]. Visit philpallen.com to explore my blog and continue learning. Got something to say? Send me a tweet @philpallen.

Now get to work.

---

[30] Hey, maybe you'll become one of my clients.

# WORKSHEETS & GLOSSARY

"You wanna live fancy? Live in a big mansion?
Party in France? You better work bitch."

@britneyspears

Sometimes you've got to get down and dirty.

To help you quickly achieve your Twitter goals, this section will train you in *Shut Up and Tweet*'s strategies. Use it wisely—and have fun.

# MINI BRAND QUESTIONNAIRE

Knowing your brand makes content creation much easier. Answering these questions will help you pinpoint and position your social media strategy.

1.  **Describe yourself in three (and only three) words.**

    _____

    _____

    _____

Now ask a few others to describe you in three words. Do they match up? They should. Before you can sell yourself, you have to know what's for sale.

2. **What do you _love_ to do?**

_____

_____

Simply put: Your brand should be something you really enjoy.

## 3. Name a few brands you look up to.

_____        _____

_____        _____

Now you can go research these brands online. Get inspired by their websites, social media platforms, color palettes, and brand positioning. Don't list Apple. Everyone does. I expect more creativity from you.

## 4. Describe your ideal customer in as much detail as possible.

_____

_____

_____

Go beyond the basics like age, sex, and location. What's his or her name? Career? Hobbies? Routine? Get painfully specific. When you try to appeal to everyone, you appeal to no one. This is your chance to concentrate on a target market that needs you.

## 5. What's your brand in one sentence?

_____

This isn't a hobby. What *need* are you satisfying? Spit it out before you lose me forever to cute videos of kitties on YouTube.

# TWEET TYPE BRAINSTORM: WEBSITE LINK (WL)

Promote yourself. Ideally link back to your website or any other relevant content.

For best results don't make your self promotion obvious. Your audience cares a lot more about themselves than they care about you, so find another way to interest them.

Examples:

How to structure your brand so you can make money. Money is good. [video] philp.al/1syXRJL

I promise my upcoming talk at @CAWomensConf will be a game changer. How to build a powerful brand. Get tickets now: bit.ly/1pzeZOf

Hey look I'm on @ThoughtCatalog! An open letter of apology on behalf of everyone who works in social media: bit.ly/1icQiEc

Need some logo inspiration? Look no further. Just added new ones on my Pinterest: philp.al/logoluv

## TWEET TYPE BRAINSTORM: QUICK QUESTION (QQ)

Engage them. Prompt users to respond and express their opinion on a brand-related topic or anything else.

For best results: Keep it short, snappy, and easy to answer. Don't always make it about your brand. You're not a robot, remember?

Examples:

Favorite song to BLAST in your headphones?

They say Pinterest outperforms Twitter and LinkedIn in the time spent on each network. Which platform do you spend the most time on?

Coffee or tea?

The best day of the week is _____ (fill in the blank).

## TWEET TYPE BRAINSTORM: INDUSTRY BUZZ (IB)

You're an expert? Prove it. Share factual information like statistics and build credibility as an industry leader.

For best results: Consider your audience's perspective. What's common sense to you might be gold to them. I often go back and listen to my recorded calls, videos, and talks and read books for tweetable tidbits.

Examples:

Your brand is only as strong as your answer to this question: What do I get from you that I can't get anywhere else[31]?

An average # of photos shared on Instagram daily? 55 mill. That's a lot of selfies.

Branding is business. Satisfy a need out there. It can't just be a hobby.

---

[31] This tweet had 15 retweets and 16 favorites. Beat that! Yes, I'm challenging you.

## TWEET TYPE BRAINSTORM: NETWORKING EFFORT (NE)

Connect with others and build rapport. Offer a thoughtful compliment to a stranger.

For best results: Try to position yourself for a retweet. Show people you care about them and you'll get something in return.

Examples:

I really can't get enough of @thedieline. Favorite blog of all time: thedieline.com

Hey @designerkelli I love your perspective on design psychology. Your book is a must-have!

I've been listening to @SamSmithWorld on repeat for months. Neighbors: I'm sorry.

# PLATFORMS & THEIR PURPOSE

No one has time for social media, so it's time to prioritize. Become a rockstar on three platforms. It's much better than being mediocre on ten.

**What three social media platforms are most important for your brand?**

    **1. Twitter**

    **2.** _____

    **3.** _____

**Honorable mentions (optional):**

    **4.** _____

    **5.** _____

These platforms get attention once you've mastered the first three.

Next: Define a purpose for your social media platforms. It establishes value for your audience, while giving you a direction for future updates.

**1. On Twitter, I'm going to:**

_____

_____

**2. On _____ , I'm going to:**

_____

_____

**3. On _____ , I'm going to:**

_____

_____

**Examples:**
- Share the newest arrivals and product giveaways.
- Curate healthy recipes or inspiring design.
- Reveal what happens behind the scenes.

# GROWTH TRACKER

Before you get carried away, let's give you a method for your madness. Use this chart (or something similar) to record your growth efforts over time. Here's how:

**Date**
Self-explanatory.

**Following**
How many people you're currently following.

**Followers**
How many people are currently following you.

**Followed**
How many people you just followed. Remember not to follow more than 300 people. Twitter sets a limit to prevent suspicious bot activity and may suspend your account.

**Hit List Account**
The account's followers you're going to steal.

**GROWTH TRACKER**

| Date | Following | Followers | Followed | Hit List Account |
|------|-----------|-----------|----------|------------------|
|      |           |           |          |                  |
|      |           |           |          |                  |
|      |           |           |          |                  |
|      |           |           |          |                  |
|      |           |           |          |                  |
|      |           |           |          |                  |
|      |           |           |          |                  |
|      |           |           |          |                  |
|      |           |           |          |                  |

# Worksheets & Glossary

# GLOSSARY

**@Reply**: A way of responding to someone who has mentioned you.

**Audience**: Future loyalists and customers.

**Authenticity**: Staying true to your brand and personality online.

**Brand heroes**: The brands who do what you do, but are a few steps ahead.

**Branding**: Establishing your recognizable identity or image.

**Business cards**: I'll hook you up.

**Call to action (CTA)**: Bossing users around. "Click here to buy my shit."

**Competitors**: Other companies in your market who are vying for your customers.

**Content calendar**: Plotting out your posts in advance like a responsible adult.

**Content**: Information you publish on social media channels.

**Content-personality ratio**: That unique mix of informative and engaging.

**Daily active users**: Number of people viewing or engaging with a social network in a given day.

**Direct competitor**: A company in your market that sells the same thing as you.

**Facebook**: A place for your friends and family, not for networking.

**Favorite:** Twitter's form of acknowledgement, manifested as a small gold star.

**Follower**: Someone who wants to see what you tweet. Don't mess this up.

**Following**: Subscribing to someone's tweets on Twitter.

**Handle**: Your username on Twitter. @philpallen, for example.

**Hit list**: The index you draft of competitors, like brands, and brand heroes whose followers may be followed by you.

**Impression**: The number of times users see your content.

**Indirect competitor**: A company in your market that sells a different product or service but satisfies the same need as yours.

**Industry buzz (IB)**: A tweet type used to establish your credibility as an expert.

**Internet**: Really?

**Internet domain registrar**: The place where you register a web URL. (GoDaddy, 1&1, name.com, etc.)

**Like brands**: Similar brands who aren't competing against you for market share.

**Logo**: Your brand's visual identifier.

**Mention**: A tweet including a username.

**Modified tweet (MT)**: Modifying someone's tweet before RTing, often adding your own thoughts to it.

**Networking effort (NE)**: A tweet type for connecting with new people.

**New-native retweet:** A way of retweeting built into Twitter's platform that keeps the tweet in its original form. Remember, you can't modify or add anything.

**Old-school retweet**: Copying and pasting a tweet and adding RT to the front before sending it.

**One-sided conversation:** Something you know better than to do anymore.

**Platform**: A fancier word for social network.

**Profile**: The online version of your high school locker.

**Profile photo**: The square photo on your Twitter profile that accompanies every tweet.

**Purchased followers**: Often fake and inactive accounts bought in the name of vanity.

**Quick question (QQ)**: A tweet type meant for engagement.

**Referrals**: Subscribing to someone's tweets on Twitter.

**Return on investment (ROI)**: Worth the money.

**Retweet (RT)**: Reposting someone's tweet to your followers.

**Social media management systems (SMMS)**: An application program that helps to successfully engage and post on social platforms.

**Social media strategy**: The plan for social media success.

**Targeted audience**: The people you're trying to reach.

**Tweet**: A message sent on Twitter. Your favorite pastime from now on.

**Tweet types**: My custom formula for a balanced content strategy: website link (WL), quick question (QQ), industry buzz (IB), and networking effort (NE).

**Twitter**: You're asking now?

**Twitterbot**: A program used to produce automated tweets through inactive accounts.

**Twittersphere**: A fancy term to describe Twitter and the users in it.

**Twitter bio:** Two sentences. First: Tell me who you are and why I should care. Second: Show your personality.

**Twitter list**: A Twitter feature that allows you to subscribe to an account without following it.

**Unfollow**: Unsubscribing from an account on Twitter to no longer receive their updates.

**Uniform resource locator (URL)**: A website or path on the Internet, ie. philpallen.com.

**Via**: A way to give credit for link sharing.

**Viral content:** Something that spreads very fast online.

**Website**: Get one.

**Website link (WL)**: A tweet type about you that ideally includes a link.

**Your new mantra**: Mistakes are better than nothing. Last time I'm telling you.

# ACKNOWLEDGEMENTS

"I just want to be humble at all times."

@MikeTyson

I realize my name is plastered all over this book, but don't let that fool you. This project was a collaborative effort, and there are a few people that deserve a shoutout.

Thank you to my hardworking writing and business partner, Lauren, who always makes my nasally vocals, filled with attitude and sass, come to life on paper. We mostly wrote this book over a series of Saturday nights alone in front of our computers, which is just sad.

Thanks to Eva, Claire and hubby Diego for gracing these pages with your presence (and edits) before it went out to the rest of the world. And Thanh, you're a wizard.

I couldn't do it without my support network (family), including Mom, Kevin, Diego, Teddy, Kristen, Gammy and Gumper. You're the best.

## ABOUT THE AUTHOR

Phil Pallen is a Los Angeles-based brand strategist. He works with personalities on major TV networks in the U.S. Phil's digital campaigns have been featured by hundreds of media outlets. When he's not on Twitter, Phil is speaking at conferences around the world about social media and branding.

@philpallen

## ABOUT THE EDITOR

Lauren Moore, also based in LA, is a content strategist who geeks out about creative writing and data crunching. Her brand experience includes MTV, BMI, DailyCandy, and Time Out New York. Lauren's social media strategies have grown companies by more than one million followers combined.

@thelaurenmoore

41683887R00059

Made in the USA
Charleston, SC
10 May 2015